INTRODUCTION

IMAGINE travelling back in time millions of years, to when giant monsters ruled planet earth. If you want to stay alive you'll have to be cool, alert – and watch your back at all times. YOU HAVE BEEN WARNED! Keep this guide handy, the information inside might just save you one day! Remember, this is no walk in the park – IT'S A PREHISTORIC JUNGLE OUT THERE!

2 IN THE BEGINNING
PREHISTORIC EARTH

Living on the planet 200 million years ago would have been a very weird experience. Climate, vegetation and wildlife were all different. During the Triassic period it was generally warm everywhere.

The age of the Dinosaurs

Triassic	245-208 MILLION YEARS AGO
Jurassic	208-144 MILLION YEARS AGO
Cretaceous	144-65 MILLION YEARS AGO

dino HUNTER

IN THE BEGINNING 3

As landmasses broke apart, creating the continents as we know them now, temperatures dropped but were still over 10° higher than today! Ferns, palms and conifers were the dominant type of vegetation, but flowers didn't appear until the Cretaceous period.

4 IN THE BEGINNING
WHAT IS A DINOSAUR?

Dinosaurs dominated the planet for over 180 million years, but not all creatures on prehistoric earth were dinosaurs. There were many other types of creature in existence from tiny insects to giant flying lizards.

What did Dinosaurs eat?

HERBIVORES plants

CARNIVORES meat

OMNIVORES meat and plants

dino HUNTER

IN THE BEGINNING 5

To be a dinosaur, a creature must:
- have lived from 245 million to 65 million years ago
- have lived on the land, not in the air or in the water
- be a reptile (although not all reptiles were dinosaurs)
- have legs located below its body, not protruding from its side (like a crocodile)

6 IN THE BEGINNING
EVIDENCE

Pterosaur fossil

Prehistoric lifeforms are often discovered fossilised in rock, but can also be found frozen in ice or trapped in amber. The very first dinosaur fossils were found in Europe, but North America is where dinosaur

Archaeopteryx fossil

IN THE BEGINNING — 7

hunting really took off. Indeed, North America has seen some of the most dramatic finds including the recent discovery of a gigantic Tyrannosaurus Rex in South Dakota. Named Sue after its finder, it is the largest and most complete Tyrannosaurus anywhere in the world – so far!

8 THE HERBIVORES
LONG NECKS

BRACHIOSAURUS

Meaning: Tall-chested arm lizard
Time: Late Jurassic
Length: 26 metres
Finds: N America; Africa; Europe.
Features: Long neck and front legs.

Long front legs helped Brachiosaurus reach twice the height of a giraffe.

THE HERBIVORES

9

dino HUNTER

BAROSAURUS

Meaning: Slow heavy lizard
Time: Late Jurassic
Length: 27 metres
Finds: NAmerica; Africa.
Features: Extremely long neck.

A real giant of the prehistoric world, Brachiosaurus is one of the most famous dinosaurs ever.

| Triassic | Jurassic | Cretaceous |

BRACHIOSAURUS, BAROSAURUS

10 THE HERBIVORES
LONG NECKS

MAMENCHISAURUS

Meaning: Lizard from Mamen Brook
Time: Late Jurassic
Length: 25 metres
Finds: China
Features: The longest neck of any known dinosaur – 14 metres.

Long necks are the perfect tool for tree grazing.

MUSSAURUS

Meaning: Mouse lizard
Time: Late Triassic
Length: 3 metres
Finds: Argentina
Features: Small head; long tail.

THE HERBIVORES

11

ASTRODON

Meaning: Sky tooth
Time: Early Cretaceous
Length: 18 metres
Finds: NAmerica
Features: Similar to Brachiosaurus.

With their heads so far from their bodies, how did these huge dinosaurs not faint? One theory is they may have had more than one heart.

Triassic	Jurassic	Cretaceous
MUSSAURUS	MAMENCHISAURUS	ASTRODON

12 THE HERBIVORES
LONG NECKS

Some long necked dinosaurs could graze large areas without needing to move.

DIPLODOCUS

Meaning: Double beam
Time: Late Jurassic
Length: 27 metres
Finds: NAmerica
Features: Neck and tail similar length.

Diplodocus may well have been a ground feeder as its front legs are shorter than its hind ones and its neck points down rather than up.

DICRAEOSAURUS

Meaning: Two forked lizard
Time: Late Jurassic
Length: 14 metres
Finds: Africa
Features: Shorter neck than most diplodocids.

THE HERBIVORES

13

Triassic | Jurassic | Cretaceous

DIPLODODUS, DICRAEOSAURUS

14 THE HERBIVORES
CLUB TAILS

The size and shape of the tail club varies greatly between dinosaur species.

EUOPLOCEPHALUS

Meaning: Well-armoured head
Time: Late Cretaceous
Length: 7 metres
Finds: NAmerica
Features: Spined back and club tail.

THE HERBIVORES

15

SHUNOSAURUS

Meaning: Shu (Sichuan) lizard
Time: Late Jurassic
Length: 10 metres
Finds: China
Features: Spiked club on tail.

Defensive tail clubs were an important part of many herbivores' weaponry.

Triassic	Jurassic	Cretaceous
	SHUNOSAURUS	EUOPLOCEPHALUS

THE HERBIVORES
SUPER SPIKERS

EDMONTONIA

Meaning: From Edmonton
Time: Late Cretaceous
Length: 7 metres
Finds: NAmerica
Features: Armoured back; huge spikes at shoulders.

KENTROSAURUS

Meaning: Pointed lizard
Time: Late Jurassic
Length: 5 metres
Finds: Africa
Features: Pairs of spikes on back and shoulders; plates on neck.

The spikes on Kentrosaurus look impressive and very dangerous.

THE HERBIVORES — 17

Like many plant-eating dinosaurs Edmontonia and Kentrosaurus may have swallowed stones to help digestion.

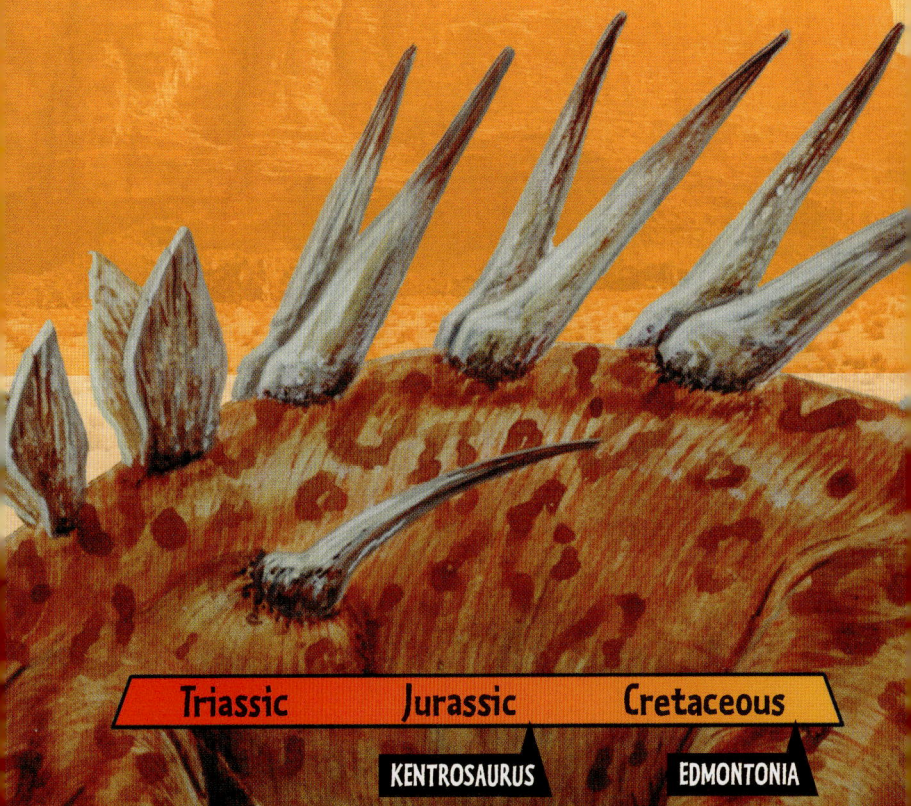

| Triassic | Jurassic | Cretaceous |

KENTROSAURUS   EDMONTONIA

THE HERBIVORES
HEAVY DUTY HORNS

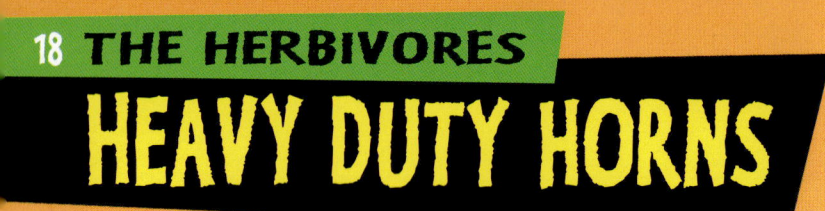

CENTROSAURUS
Meaning: Pointed lizard
Time: Late Cretaceous
Length: 6 metres
Finds: NAmerica
Features: Large single snout horn; large neck shield with cut-outs.

TRICERATOPS
Meaning: Three-horned face
Time: Late Cretaceous
Length: 9 metres
Finds: NAmerica
Features: Three skull horns; large neck shield.

THE HERBIVORES

19

dino HUNTER

This group of dinosaurs are ancestors to the modern-day rhinoceros.

STYRACOSAURUS

Meaning: Spiked lizard
Time: Late Cretaceous
Length: 5.5 metres
Finds: NAmerica
Features: Array of horns on edge of neck shield; massive nose horn.

The aggressive looking headgear was actually for defensive purposes.

| Triassic | Jurassic | Cretaceous |

TRICERATOPS, CENTROSAURUS, STYRACOSAURUS

20 THE HERBIVORES
ARMOUR PLATED

STEGOSAURUS

Meaning: Roof lizard
Time: Late Jurassic
Length: 9 metres
Finds: N America; Europe.
Features: Huge alternating plates along back; small spikes on tail.

Heat regulating plates are the most distinctive feature of Stegosaurus.

Triassic	Jurassic	Cretaceous
	STEGOSAURUS, TUOJIANGOSAURUS	WUERHOSAURUS

THE HERBIVORES

21

One of the most recognisable of all dinosaurs, Stegosaurus evolved in China before migrating to Africa and North America.

WUERHOSAURUS

Meaning: Wuerho lizard
Time: Early Cretaceous
Length: 8 metres
Finds: China
Features: Double row of back plates; tail spikes.

TUOJIANGOSAURUS

Meaning: Lizard from Tuo river
Time: Late Jurassic
Length: 7 metres
Finds: China
Features: Pairs of pointed plates along back; small spikes on tail.

22 THE HERBIVORES
HORNBLOWERS

PARASAUROLOPHUS
Meaning: Almost crested lizard
Time: Late Cretaceous
Length: 10 metres
Finds: NAmerica
Features: Flamboyant curved head crest.

SAUROLOPHUS
Meaning: Lizard crest
Time: Late Cretaceous
Length: 12 metres
Finds: NAmerica
Features: Spine rising above eyes.

23

THE HERBIVORES

dino HUNTER

A loud and clear alarm signal could be a real life-saver.

HYPACROSAURUS

Meaning: Below the top lizard
Time: Late Cretaceous
Length: 9 metres
Finds: NAmerica
Features: Thick head crest.

Some Hadrosaurs had fantastic head crests and large nasal passages for visual and audible signalling.

| Triassic | Jurassic | Cretaceous |

PARASAUROLOPHUS, SAUROLOPHUS, HYPACROSAURUS

24 THE HERBIVORES
SMALL & SPEEDY

DRYOSAURUS

Meaning: Oak lizard
Time: Late Jurassic
Length: 4 metres
Finds: NAmerica
Features: Sturdy legs; hardedged, beak-like mouth.

LEAELLYNASAURA

Meaning: Leaellyn's lizard
Time: Mid Cretaceous
Length: 3 metres
Finds: Australia
Features: Large eye sockets.

DINO FACTS
DID YOU KNOW?

...that there were even bigger dinosaurs than T.Rex? Giganotosaurus from Patagonia had longer and heavier thigh bones. Carcharodontosaurus (shark tooth lizard) from the Sahara had a skull over 5 feet (1.62m) long.

...that the biggest flying creature that ever lived was a dinosaur called Quetzalcoatlus? This mega-vulture had a wingspan of 50 feet (15.4 metres). Its hollow bones were as light as styrofoam.

...that during most of the Age of the Dinosaurs there were no flowers? Until the end of the Cretaceous Period, nearly all land plants were either conifers or ferns.

RE-USABLE in the dark GLOW STICKERS

DINO FACTS
DID YOU KNOW?

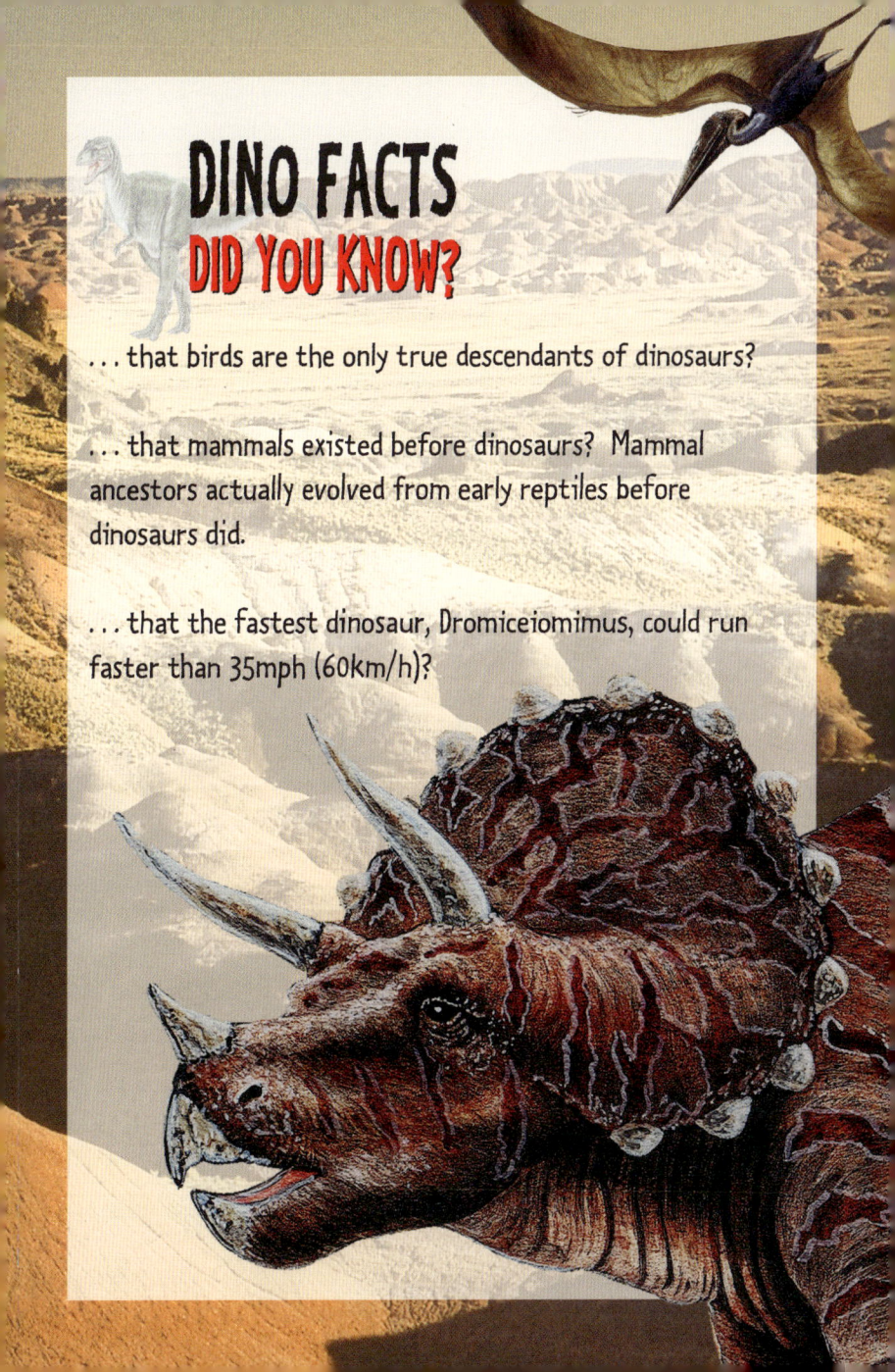

... that birds are the only true descendants of dinosaurs?

... that mammals existed before dinosaurs? Mammal ancestors actually evolved from early reptiles before dinosaurs did.

... that the fastest dinosaur, Dromiceiomimus, could run faster than 35mph (60km/h)?

RE-USABLE in the dark GLOW STICKERS

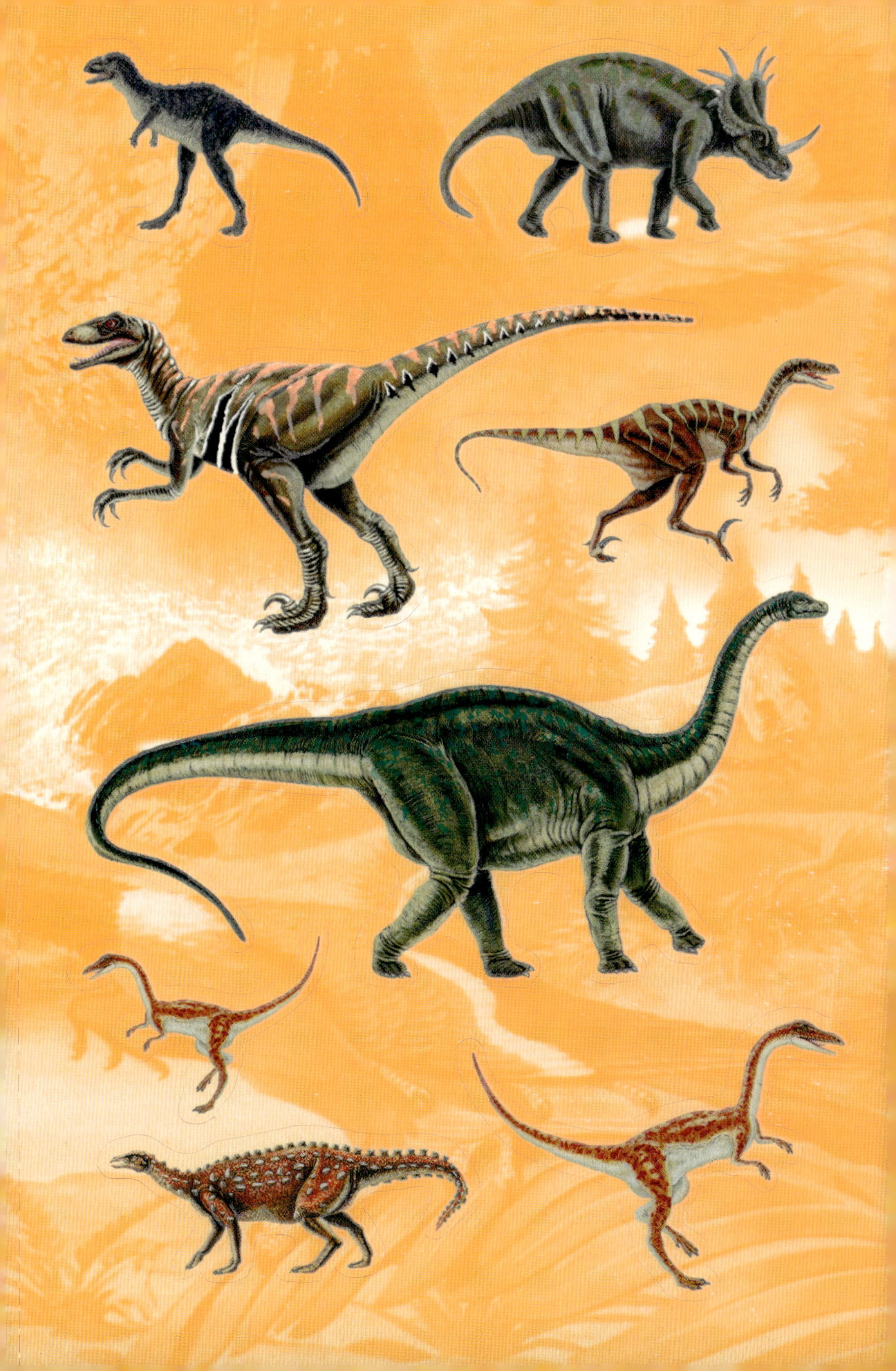

DINO FACTS
DID YOU KNOW?

... that more than nine different kinds of dinosaur egg have been found?

... that some dinosaurs had feathers but could not fly?

... that fossils are not all bones or teeth? A chunk of fossilised dino dung almost three litres in size has been found in Saskatchewan, USA? From its age, size and contents, scientists guess it came from T.Rex.

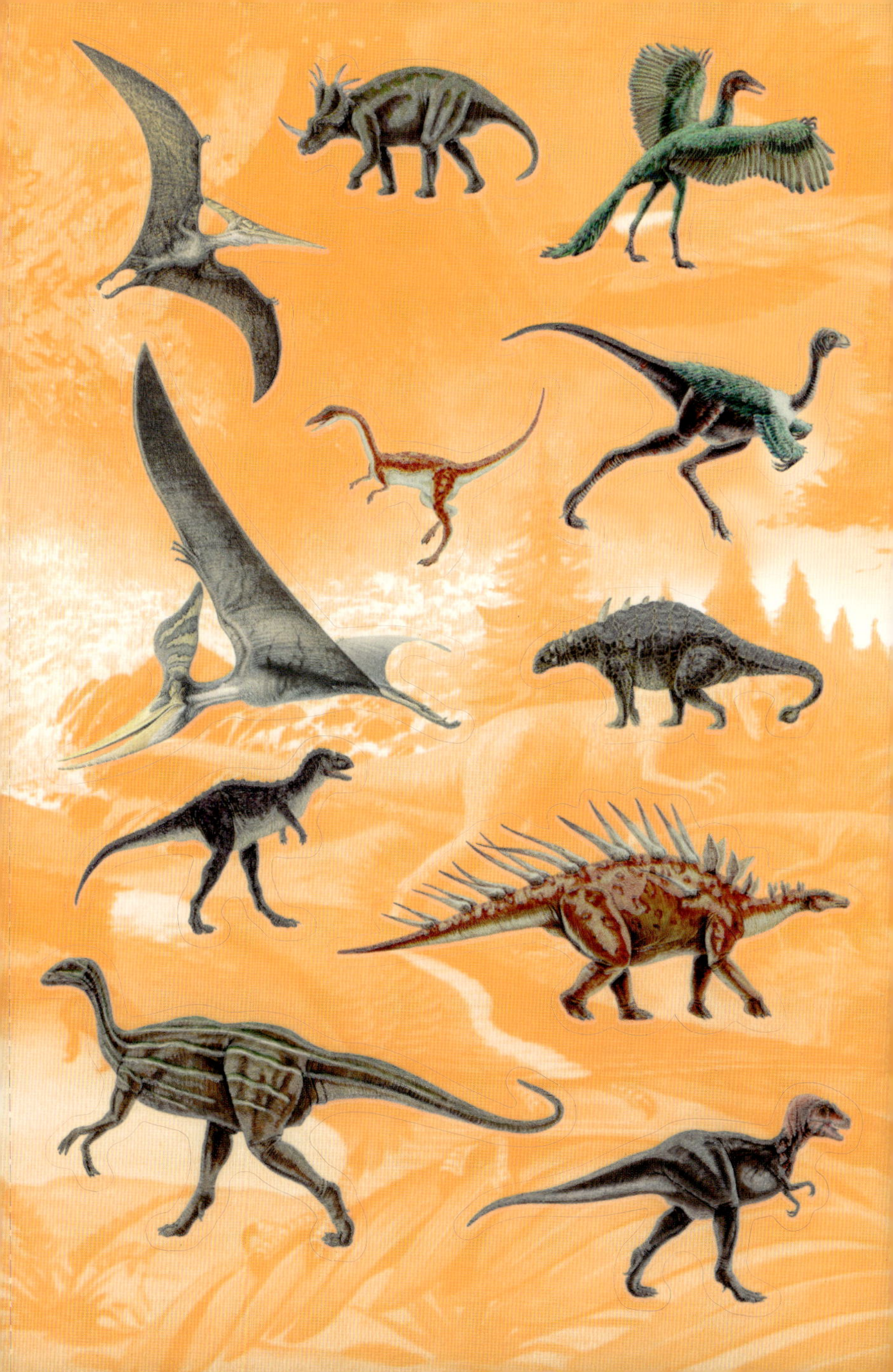

DINO FACTS
DID YOU KNOW?

... that the remains of about 2100 different species of dinosaur can be seen in the world's museums?

... that the first dinosaur to be reconstructed was an Iguanodon? To begin with, its long, pointed claw was placed on its nose, like a rhino horn!

... that nobody knows what a dinosaur heart looks like?

... that the oldest true dinosaur found so far is Herrerasaurus, discovered in Argentina in 1989? This two-legged, two metre tall species lived nearly 230 million years ago.

THE HERBIVORES

These creatures were the dinosaur world's equivalent of early gazelles and antelopes.

HYPSILOPHODON

Meaning: High-ridged tooth
Time: Mid Cretaceous
Length: 2.3 metres
Finds: Europe
Features: Fast – long legs and lightweight.

Eventually they became commonplace, and examples of this group have been found on almost every continent.

Triassic	Jurassic	Cretaceous
	DRYOSAURUS	HYPSILOPHODON, LEAELLYNASAURA

26 THE CARNIVORES
FAST ATTACKERS

VELOCIRAPTOR

Meaning: Fast hunter
Time: Late Cretaceous
Length: 4 metres
Finds: Mongolia; China.
Features: Eagle-like talons; curved killing claw.

COELURUS

Meaning: Hollow tail
Time: Late Jurassic
Length: 2 metres
Finds: NAmerica
Features: Sharp, curved teeth.

27

THE CARNIVORES

Intelligence and teamwork make these predatory dinosaurs some of the most feared.

DEINONYCHUS

Meaning: Terrible claw
Time: Early Cretaceous
Length: 4 metres
Finds: NAmerica
Features: Killer claw on hind feet.

They were a serious threat to even the largest herbivores.

Triassic	Jurassic	Cretaceous
	COELURUS	DEINONYCHUS	VELOCIRAPTOR

28 THE CARNIVORES
FAST ATTACKERS

COELOPHYSIS

Meaning: Hollow form
Time: Late Triassic
Length: 3 metres
Finds: NAmerica
Features: Lightweight running hunter; strong skull and neck.

Large eyes indicate they may have been well suited to hunting at night.

Triassic	Jurassic	Cretaceous
COELOPHYSIS		TROODON, DROMAEOSAURUS

THE CARNIVORES

Unusually large brains were a feature of this group.

DROMAEOSAURUS

Meaning: Running lizard
Time: Late Cretaceous
Length: 1.8 metres
Finds: NAmerica
Features: Long jaws, deep rounded snout.

TROODON

Meaning: Tearing tooth
Time: Late Cretaceous
Length: 1.8 metres
Finds: NAmerica
Features: Long head; big eyes; largest brain-body ratio.

30 THE CARNIVORES
FAST ATTACKERS

BARYONYX

Meaning: Heavy claw
Time: Early Cretaceous
Length: 9 metres
Finds: Europe
Features: Narrow jaw; small teeth; front legs armed with heavy claw.

Evidence suggests that Baryonyx enjoyed a mainly fish diet.

Triassic	Jurassic	Cretaceous
DILOPHOSAURUS	ORNITHOLESTES	BARYONYX

THE CARNIVORES

Some hunted in packs, thereby increasing the chances of a successful kill.

DILOPHOSAURUS

Meaning: Lizard with two crests
Time: Early Jurassic
Length: 6 metres
Finds: NAmerica; China
Features: Pair of semi-circular crests.

ORNITHOLESTES

Meaning: Bird thief
Time: Late Jurassic
Length: 2 metres
Finds: NAmerica
Features: Long tail; small, bony snout crest.

32 THE CARNIVORES
MEAT-EATING GIANTS

YANGCHUANOSAURUS

Meaning: Yangchuan lizard
Time: Late Jurassic
Length: 10 metres
Finds: China
Features: More teeth than Allosaurus.

TYRANNOSAURUS

Meaning: Tyrant lizard
Time: Late Cretaceous
Length: 14 metres
Finds: Mongolia; N America.
Features: Short, deep skull; good hearing.

These carnivores are amongst the most awe-inspiring of the dinosaur age.

THE CARNIVORES — 33

dino HUNTER

ALLOSAURUS

Meaning: Different lizard
Time: Late Jurassic
Length: 12 metres
Finds: NAmerica; Australia; Africa.
Features: Massive hind legs; huge head; serrated teeth.

Allosaurs may have been the largest carnivores ever to have lived on land.

Triassic	Jurassic	Cretaceous
	YANGCHUANOSAURUS, ALLOSAURUS	TYRANNOSAURUS

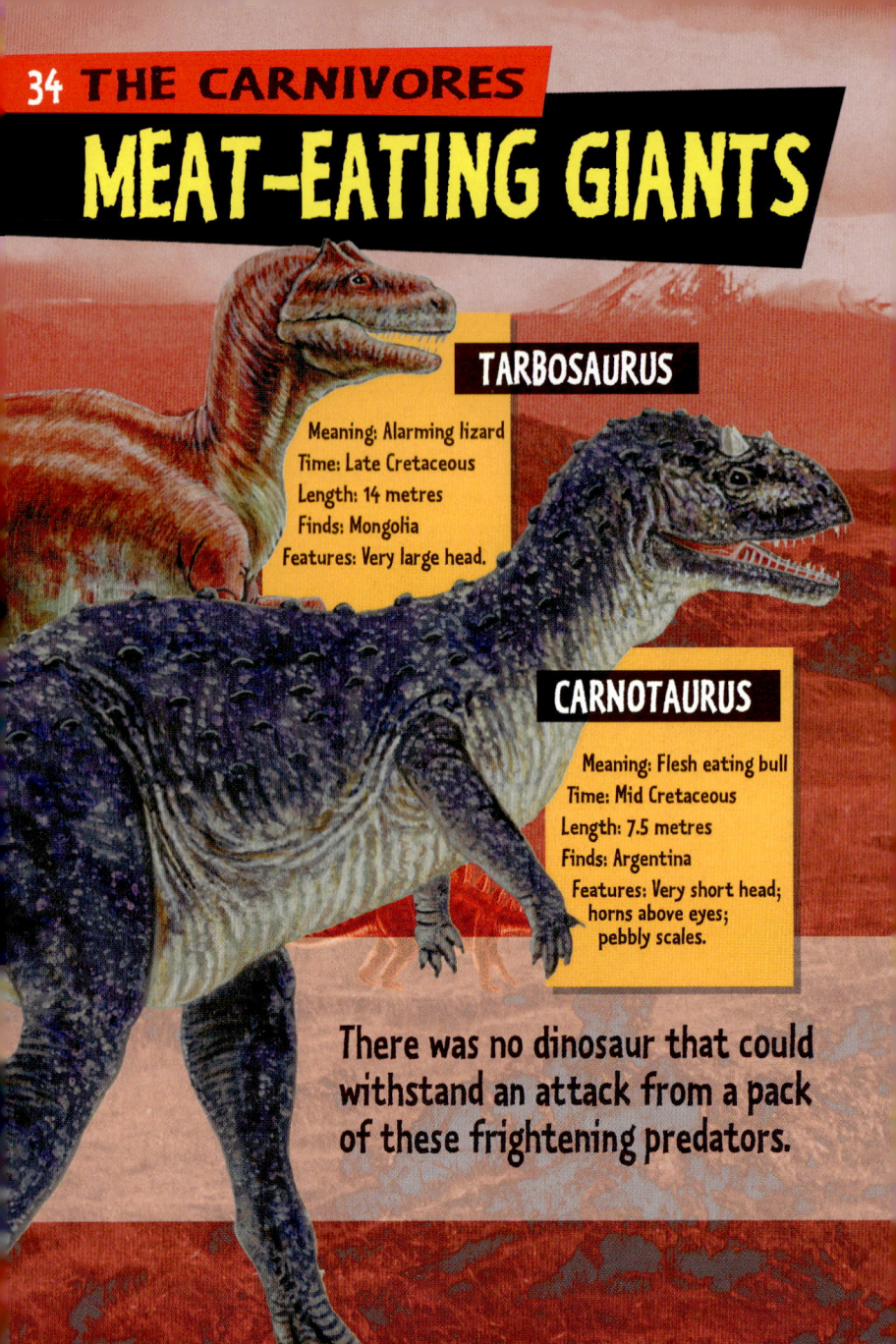

34 THE CARNIVORES
MEAT-EATING GIANTS

TARBOSAURUS

Meaning: Alarming lizard
Time: Late Cretaceous
Length: 14 metres
Finds: Mongolia
Features: Very large head.

CARNOTAURUS

Meaning: Flesh eating bull
Time: Mid Cretaceous
Length: 7.5 metres
Finds: Argentina
Features: Very short head; horns above eyes; pebbly scales.

There was no dinosaur that could withstand an attack from a pack of these frightening predators.

dino HUNTER

35

THE CARNIVORES

CERATOSAURUS

Meaning: Horned lizard
Time: Late Jurassic
Length: 6 metres
Finds: NAmerica
Features: Pronounced horns on the head.

Powerful jaws and serrated teeth – perfect weapons for a prehistoric predator.

Triassic	Jurassic	Cretaceous
	CERATOSAURUS	CARNOTAURUS	TARBOSAURUS

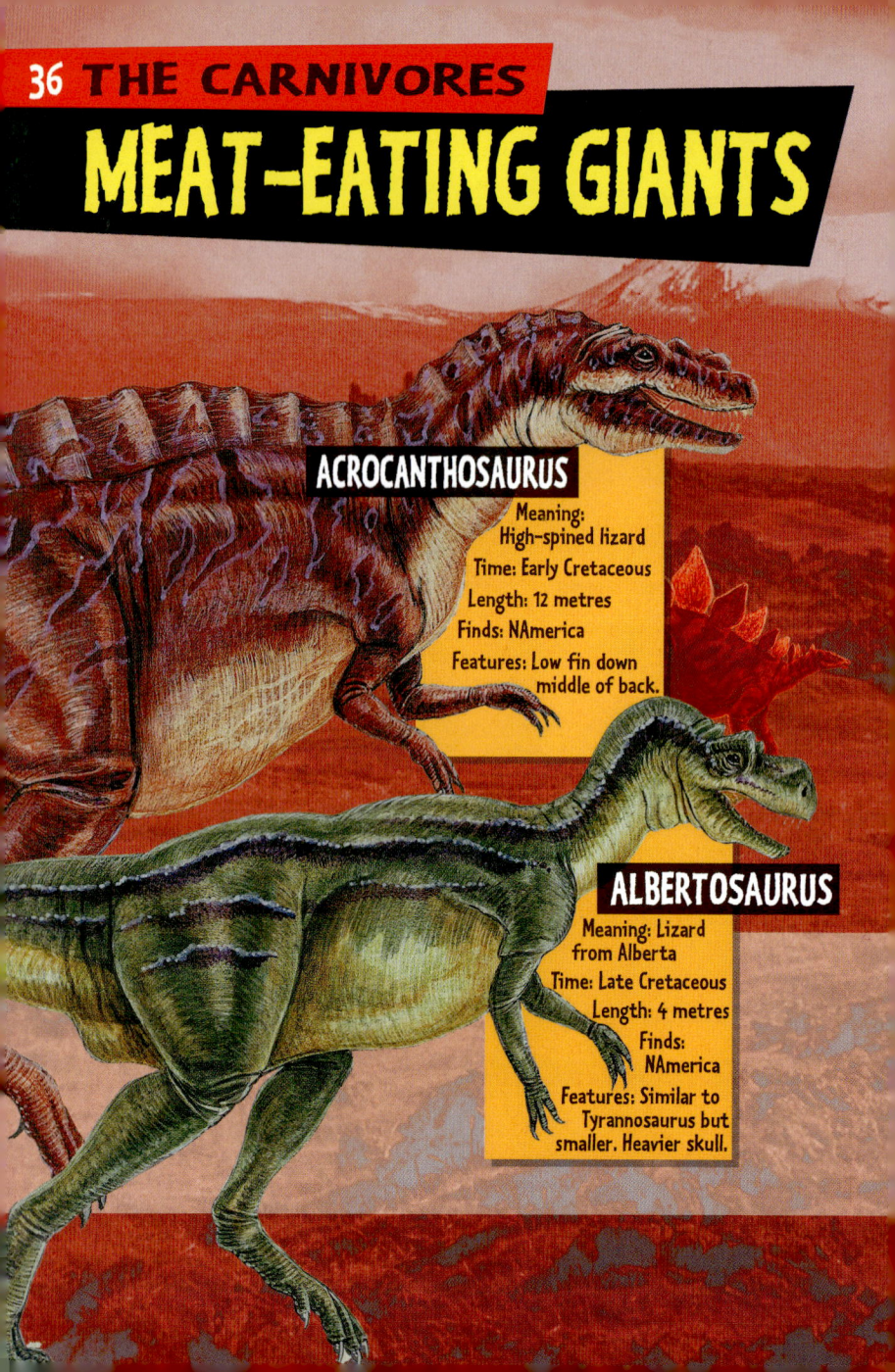

36 THE CARNIVORES
MEAT-EATING GIANTS

ACROCANTHOSAURUS
Meaning: High-spined lizard
Time: Early Cretaceous
Length: 12 metres
Finds: NAmerica
Features: Low fin down middle of back.

ALBERTOSAURUS
Meaning: Lizard from Alberta
Time: Late Cretaceous
Length: 4 metres
Finds: NAmerica
Features: Similar to Tyrannosaurus but smaller. Heavier skull.

These carnivores would also have scavenged for dead remains.

dino HUNTER

37

THE CARNIVORES

EUSTREPTOSPONDYLUS

Meaning: Curved spine
Time: Mid Jurassic
Length: 7 metres
Finds: England
Features: Curved spine, hence name.

Weighing in at 3 tons Albertosaurus was one of the smallest of this group, but it was still bigger than any predatory land animal alive today.

Triassic	Jurassic	Cretaceous
EUSTREPTOSPONDYUS	ACROCANTHOSAURUS	ALBERTOSAURUS

38 THE CARNIVORES
MEAT-EATING GIANTS

Sails are a very useful aid to heat regulation but are really quite rare.

SPINOSAURUS
Meaning: Spined lizard
Time: Late Cretaceous
Length: 16 metres
Finds: Africa
Features: Temperature regulating sail.

Spinosaurus is one of a small list of land-based dinosaur fish eaters.

Triassic	Jurassic	Cretaceous
	MEGALOSAURUS	SPINOSAURUS, DEINOCHEIRUS

39

THE CARNIVORES

DEINOCHEIRUS

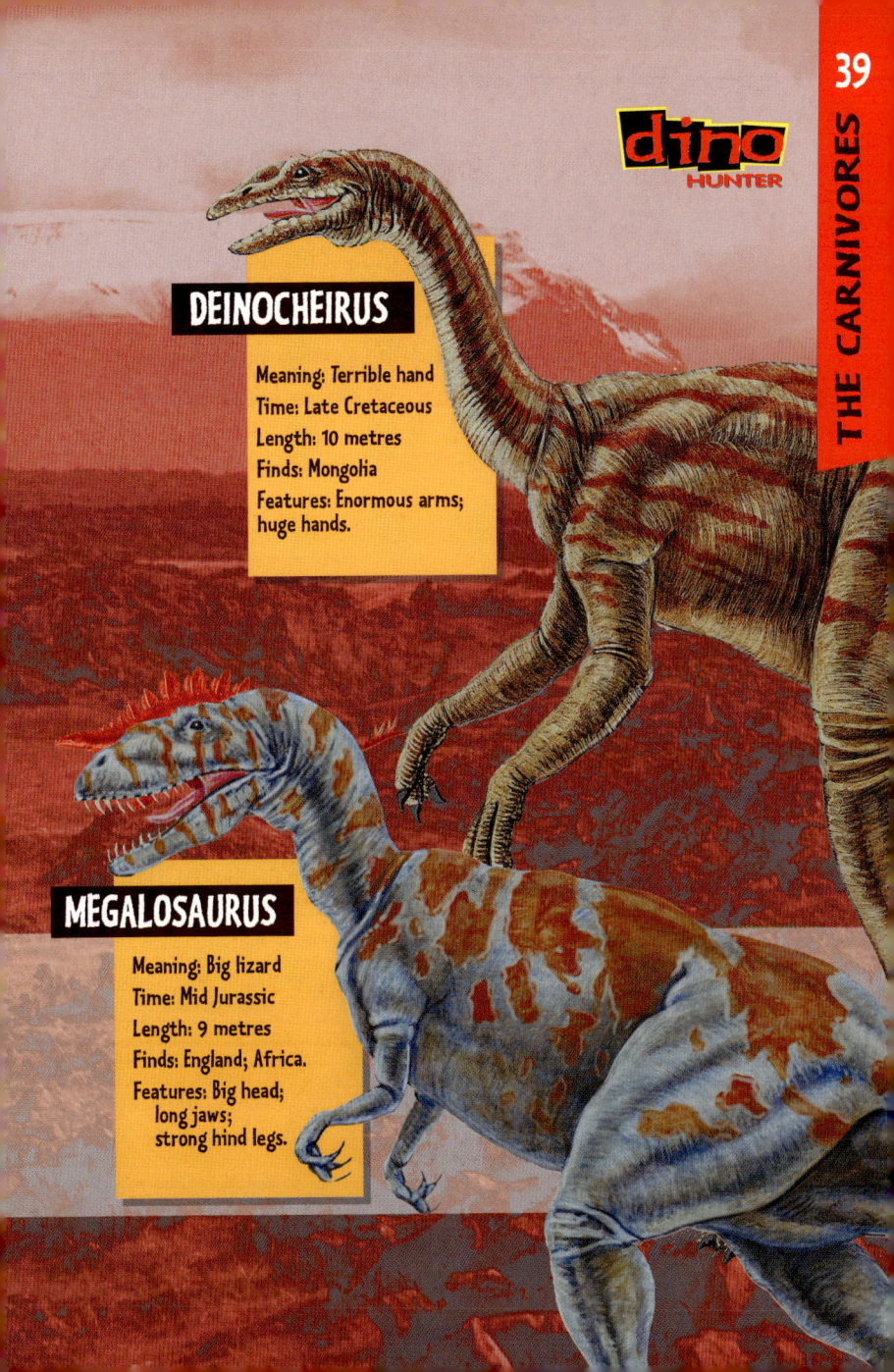

Meaning: Terrible hand
Time: Late Cretaceous
Length: 10 metres
Finds: Mongolia
Features: Enormous arms; huge hands.

MEGALOSAURUS

Meaning: Big lizard
Time: Mid Jurassic
Length: 9 metres
Finds: England; Africa.
Features: Big head; long jaws; strong hind legs.

40 THE OMNIVORES
EARLY BIRDS

SEGNOSAURUS

Meaning: Slow lizard
Time: Cretaceous
Length: 4-9 metres
Finds: Asia
Features: Toothless beak; small needle-like teeth at back of jaw.

ARCHAEORNITHOMIMUS

Meaning: Early bird mimic
Time: Cretaceous
Length: 3.5 metres
Finds: Mongolia
Features: Fast runner.

THE OMNIVORES

41

Omnivores evolved to survive feeding on both meat and vegetation.

OVIRAPTOR

Meaning: Egg stealer
Time: Late Cretaceous
Length: 2.5 metres
Finds: Mongolia
Features: Large display crest.

Oviraptor may have been incorrectly named – not thieving eggs as was thought, but sitting on them as in recent finds.

Triassic	Jurassic	Cretaceous
	ARCHAEORNITHOMIMUS, SEGNOSAURUS	OVIRAPTOR

42

THE OMNIVORES
EARLY BIRDS

GARUDIMIMUS
Meaning: Garuda (indian deity) mimic
Time: Cretaceous
Length: 4 metres
Finds: Mongolia
Features: Small head crest.

Long, powerful legs were a common feature of these dinosaurs.

DROMICEIOMIMUS
Meaning: Emu mimic
Time: Cretaceous
Length: 3.5 metres
Finds: NAmerica
Features: Big eyes; 40mph running speed.

dino HUNTER

43

THE OMNIVORES

GALLIMIMUS

Meaning: Chicken mimic
Time: Cretaceous
Length: 6 metres
Finds: Asia
Features: Tall; light.

Gallimimus was the prehistoric version of a large ostrich.

Triassic | Jurassic | **Cretaceous**

GARUDIMIMUS, DROMICEIOMIMUS, GALLIMIMUS

44 THE PTEROSAURS
FLYING REPTILES

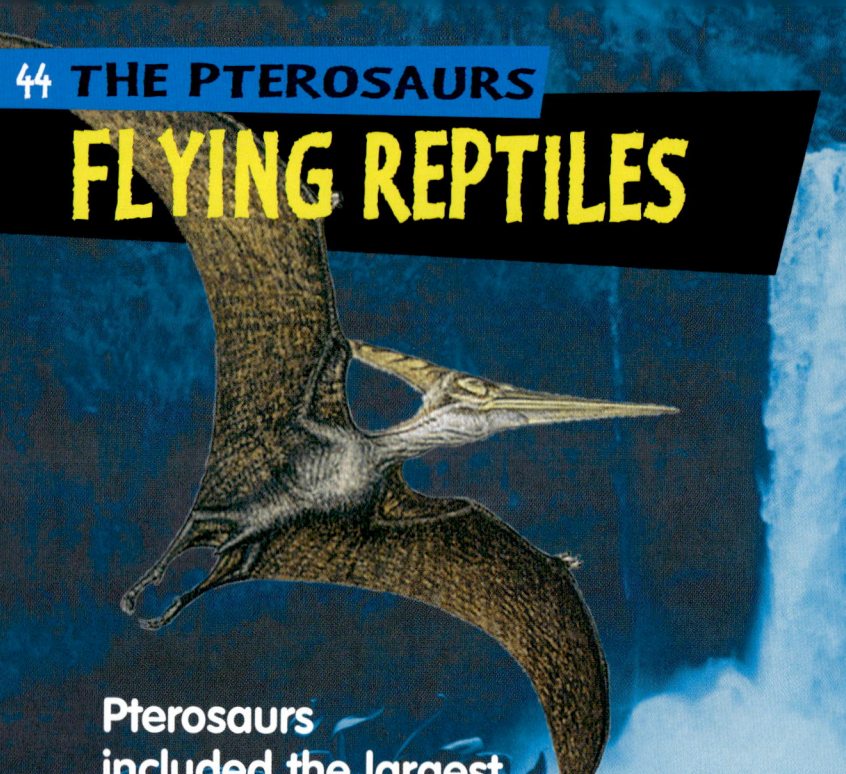

Pterosaurs included the largest creatures ever to take to the skies.

The first flying reptiles appeared over 240 million years ago, simply gliding between trees. Time and evolution eventually brought the Pterosaurs, which took to the air on wings of skin. They ruled the skies while dinosaurs ruled the land.

| Triassic | Jurassic | Cretaceous |

PTERANODON

PTERANODON

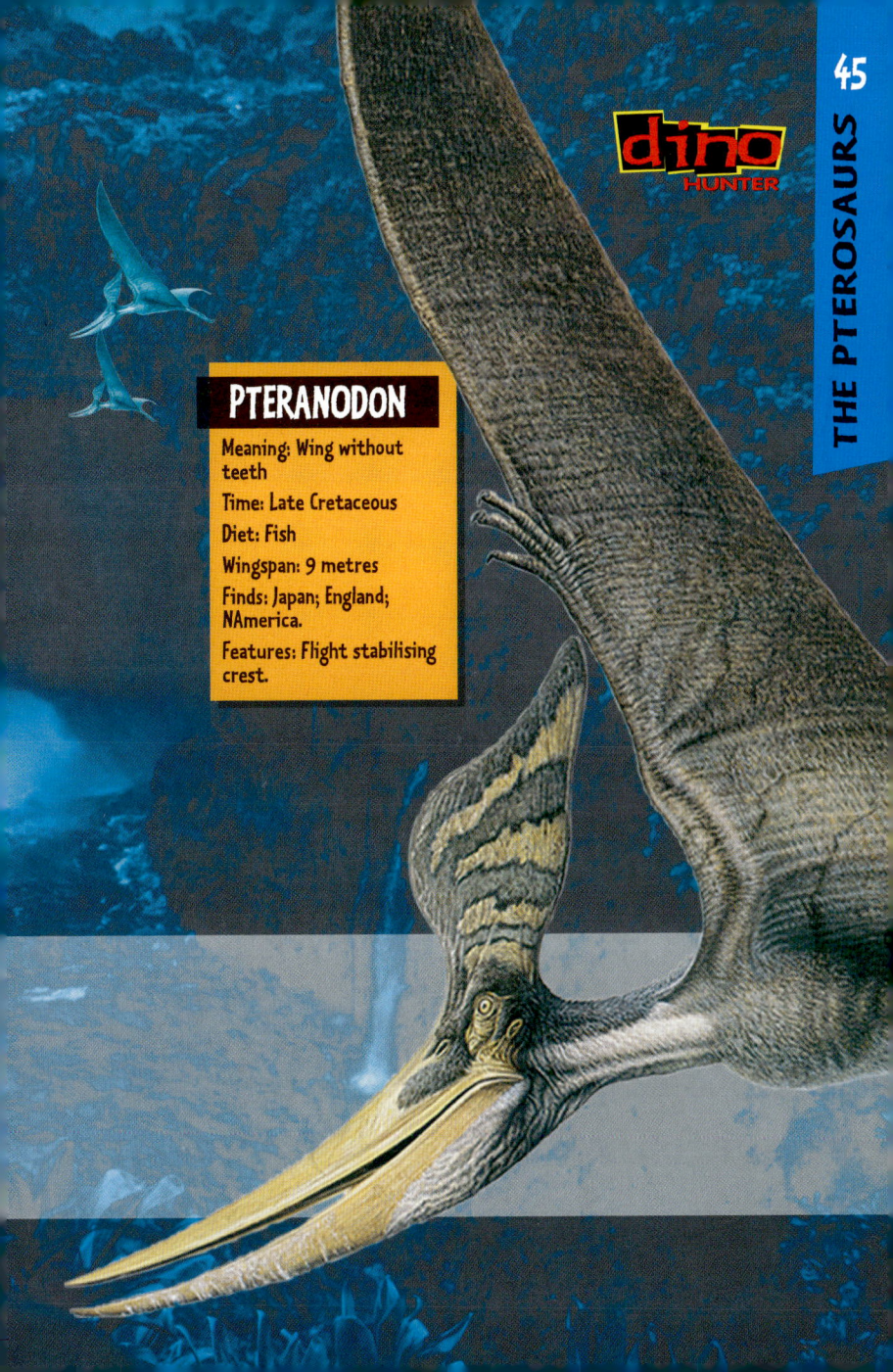

Meaning: Wing without teeth
Time: Late Cretaceous
Diet: Fish
Wingspan: 9 metres
Finds: Japan; England; NAmerica.
Features: Flight stabilising crest.

THE PTEROSAURS

45

46 THE PTEROSAURS
FLYING REPTILES

BATRACHOGNATHUS

Meaning: Frog jaw
Time: Late Jurassic
Diet: Insects
Wingspan: 50 centimetres
Finds: Asia
Features: Deep, blunt beak.

Pterosaurs – the airborne equivalent of dinosaurs.

47

THE PTEROSAURS

PTERODACTYL

Meaning: Winged finger
Time: Late Jurassic
Diet: Fish
Wingspan: 2.5 metres
Finds: Africa; Europe
Features: Compact body; long wings; short tail.

Some Pterodactyls were no larger than pigeons while others were the largest flying creatures ever to have existed.

| Triassic | Jurassic | Cretaceous |

BATRACHOGNATHUS, PTERODACTYL

The age of the Dinosaurs